ALBUM IV

6 Easy Pieces for Treble (Alto) Recorder and Basso continuo
by J. S. Bach, F. Barsanti, Ph. de Lavigne,
and M. Zimmermann

Edited by
Manfredo Zimmermann

DOWANI International

Preface

This edition offers easy-to-play yet musically challenging arrangements for treble (alto) recorder and basso continuo. Manfredo Zimmermann, professor of recorder at the Musikhochschule Cologne/Wuppertal and specialist in early music has edited and performed this collection of musical highlights from several different European countries. The basso continuo accompaniment is set for different instruments in the individual pieces and is performed on harpsichord or organ in the recordings.

The CD opens with the concert version of each piece, played with recorder and basso continuo. After tuning your instrument (Track 1), you can set to work. Your first practice session should begin at the slow tempo. If your stereo system is equipped with a balance control, you can, by turning the control, smoothly blend either the recorder or the harpsichord (or organ) accompaniment into the foreground. However, the recorder will always remain audible in the background, even if very softly. In the middle position, both instruments can be heard at the same volume. If you do not have a balance control, you can listen to the solo instrument on one loudspeaker and the accompaniment on the other. Having mastered the piece at slow tempo, you can now practice it at medium tempo. We have decided against offering the "Ariette" by Philippe de Lavigne at a moderate tempo, since the original is relatively slow. Then you can advance to the original tempo, with accompaniment. At both the medium and original tempos, the continuo can be heard in stereo quality on both channels (without the recorder). All of the versions were recorded live. The names of the musicians are listed on the last page of this volume; further information can be found in the Internet at www.dowani.com.

We wish you lots of fun playing from our *DOWANI 3 Tempi Play Along* editions and hope that your musicality and diligence will enable you to play the concert version as soon as possible. Our goal is to provide the essential conditions you need for effective practicing through motivation, enjoyment and fun.

Your DOWANI Team

Avant-propos

Le présent recueil vous propose des arrangements pour flûte à bec alto et basse continue qui sont techniquement faciles, mais d'un haut niveau musical. Manfredo Zimmermann, professeur de flûte à bec au Conservatoire Supérieur de Cologne/Wuppertal et spécialiste dans le domaine de la musique ancienne, a édité et enregistré cette collection de morceaux célèbres de plusieurs pays européen. L'instrumentation de la basse continue est différente pour chaque morceau ; elle a été enregistrée avec clavecin ou bien orgue.

Le CD vous permettra d'entendre d'abord la version de concert de chaque morceau (flûte à bec et basse continue). Après avoir accordé votre instrument (plage n° 1), vous pourrez commencer le travail musical. Le premier contact avec les morceaux devrait se faire à un tempo lent. Si votre chaîne hi-fi dispose d'un réglage de balance, vous pouvez l'utiliser pour mettre au premier plan soit la flûte à bec, soit l'accompagnement au clavecin ou bien à l'orgue. La flûte à bec restera cependant toujours audible très doucement à l'arrière-plan. En équilibrant la balance, vous entendrez les deux instruments à volume égal. Si vous ne disposez pas de réglage de balance, vous entendrez l'instrument soliste sur un des haut-parleurs et l'accompagnement sur l'autre. Après avoir étudié les morceaux à un tempo lent, vous pourrez les travailler à un tempo modéré. Nous nous sommes abstenus d'enregistrer l'"Ariette" de Philippe de Lavigne, car son tempo original est déjà relativement lent. Vous pourrez ensuite jouer le tempo original. Dans ces deux tempos vous entendrez l'accompagnement de la basse continue sur les deux canaux en stéréo (sans la partie de flûte à bec). Toutes les versions ont été enregistrées en direct. Vous trouverez les noms des artistes qui ont participé aux enregistrements sur la dernière page de cette édition ; pour obtenir plus de renseignements, veuillez consulter notre site Internet : www.dowani.com.

Nous vous souhaitons beaucoup de plaisir à faire de la musique avec la collection *DOWANI 3 Tempi Play Along* et nous espérons que votre musicalité et votre application vous amèneront aussi rapidement que possible à la version de concert. Notre but est de vous offrir les bases nécessaires pour un travail efficace par la motivation et le plaisir.

Les Éditions DOWANI

Vorwort

Mit dieser Ausgabe stellen wir Ihnen leichte, aber musikalisch anspruchsvolle Bearbeitungen für Altblockflöte und Basso continuo vor. Manfredo Zimmermann, Professor für Blockflöte an der Musikhochschule Köln/Wuppertal und Spezialist für Alte Musik, hat die vorliegende Sammlung musikalischer Highlights aus verschiedenen europäischen Ländern herausgegeben und eingespielt. Die Basso-continuo-Begleitung ist bei den einzelnen Stücken unterschiedlich besetzt und wurde mit Cembalo oder Orgel eingespielt.

Auf der CD können Sie zuerst die Konzertversion eines jeden Stückes anhören (Blockflöte und Basso continuo). Nach dem Stimmen Ihres Instrumentes (Track 1) kann die musikalische Arbeit beginnen. Ihr erster Übe-Kontakt mit den Stücken sollte im langsamen Tempo stattfinden. Wenn Ihre Stereoanlage über einen Balance-Regler verfügt, können Sie durch Drehen des Reglers entweder die Blockflöte oder die Cembalo- bzw. Orgelbegleitung stufenlos in den Vordergrund blenden. Die Blockflöte bleibt jedoch immer – wenn auch sehr leise – hörbar. In der Mittelposition erklingen beide Instrumente gleich laut. Falls Sie keinen Balance-Regler haben, hören Sie das Soloinstrument auf dem einen Lautsprecher, die Begleitung auf dem anderen. Nachdem Sie die Stücke im langsamen Tempo einstudiert haben, können Sie diese auch im mittleren Tempo üben. Bei der „Ariette" von Philippe de Lavigne haben wir auf das mittlere Tempo verzichtet, da sie im Original schon relativ langsam ist. Anschließend können Sie sich im Originaltempo begleiten lassen. Die Basso-continuo-Begleitung erklingt im mittleren und originalen Tempo auf beiden Kanälen (ohne Blockflöte) in Stereo-Qualität. Alle eingespielten Versionen wurden live aufgenommen. Die Namen der Künstler finden Sie auf der letzten Seite dieser Ausgabe; ausführlichere Informationen können Sie im Internet unter www.dowani.com nachlesen.

Wir wünschen Ihnen viel Spaß beim Musizieren mit unseren *DOWANI 3 Tempi Play Along*-Ausgaben und hoffen, dass Ihre Musikalität und Ihr Fleiß Sie möglichst bald bis zur Konzertversion führen werden. Unser Ziel ist es, Ihnen durch Motivation, Freude und Spaß die notwendigen Voraussetzungen für effektives Üben zu schaffen.

Ihr DOWANI Team

Menuet I

J. S. Bach

DOW 2523

Menuet II

J. S. Bach

6

Gavotta

from Sonata in G-minor

F. Barsanti

Recorder

Basso continuo

Ariette

from "La Beaumont"

Ph. de Lavigne

Recorder

Basso continuo

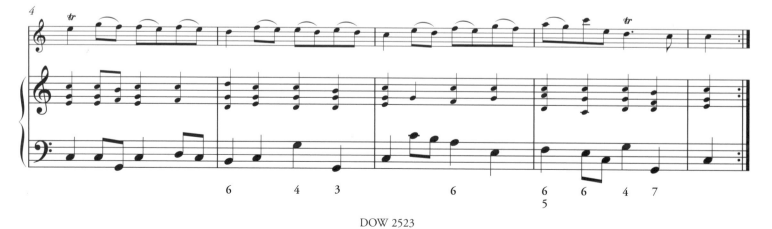

Recorder

6 Easy Pieces

for Treble (Alto) Recorder and Basso continuo

Edited by M. Zimmermann

Menuet I

J. S. Bach

Menuet II

J. S. Bach

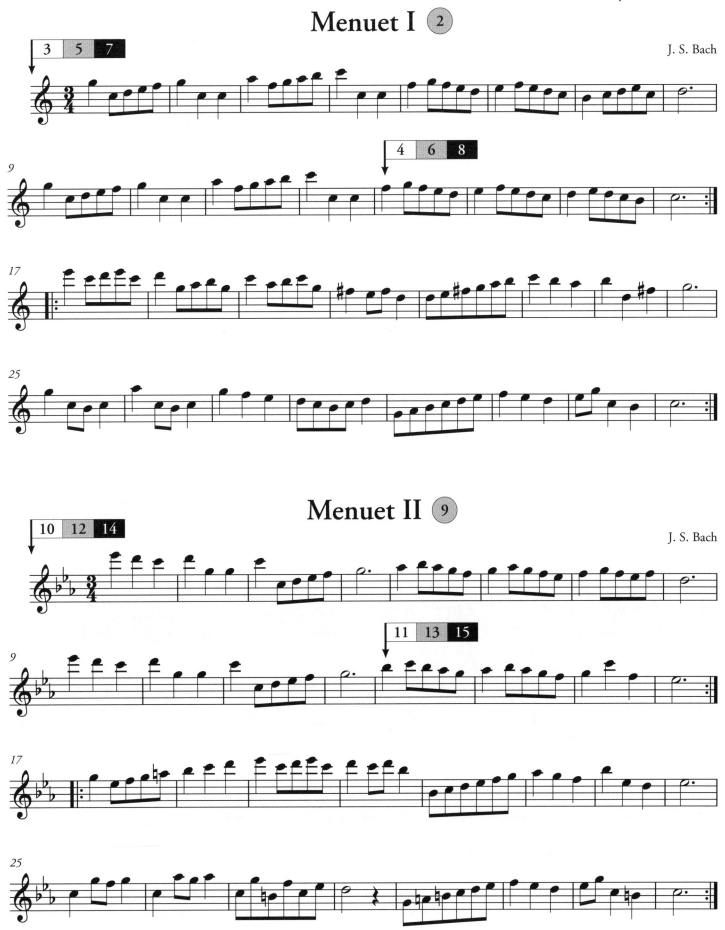

DOW 2523

Gavotta (16)

from Sonata in G-minor

F. Barsanti

Ariette (23)

from "La Beaumont"

Ph. de Lavigne

Gracieusement 28

from "La Simianne"

Ph. de Lavigne

4

Passacaglia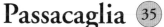

M. Zimmermann

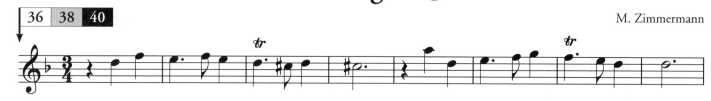

Basso continuo

6 Easy Pieces
for Treble (Alto) Recorder and Basso continuo

Edited by M. Zimmermann

Menuet I

J. S. Bach

Menuet II

J. S. Bach

DOW 2523

2

Gavotta

from Sonata in G-minor

F. Barsanti

Ariette

from "La Beaumont"

Ph. de Lavigne

Gracieusement

from "La Simianne"

Ph. de Lavigne

Passacaglia

M. Zimmermann

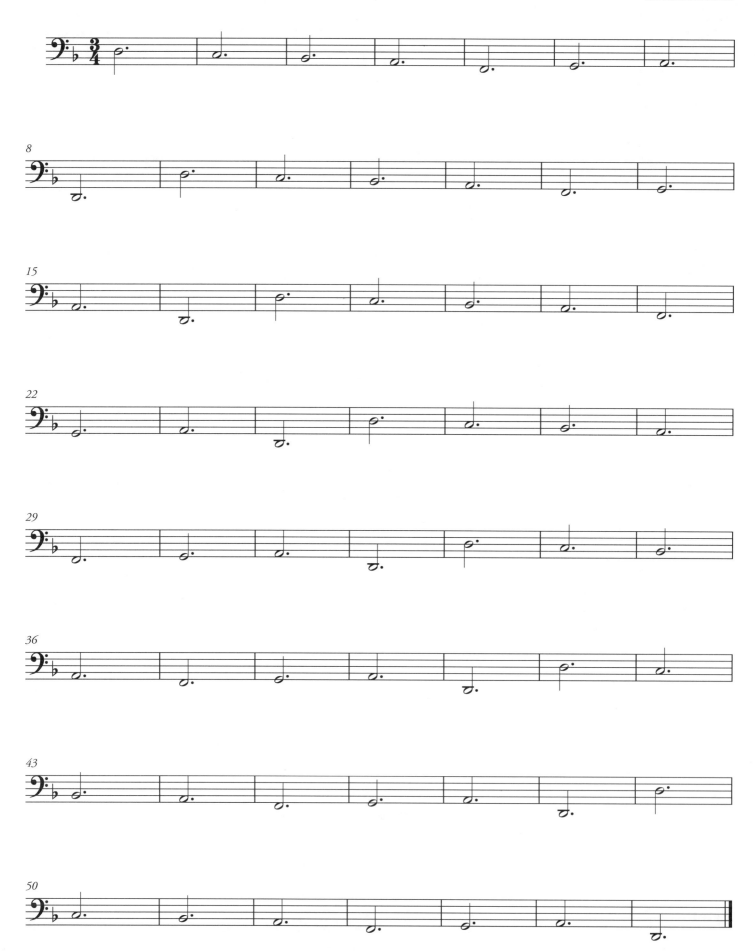

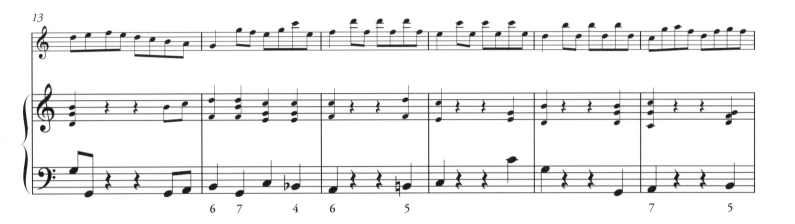

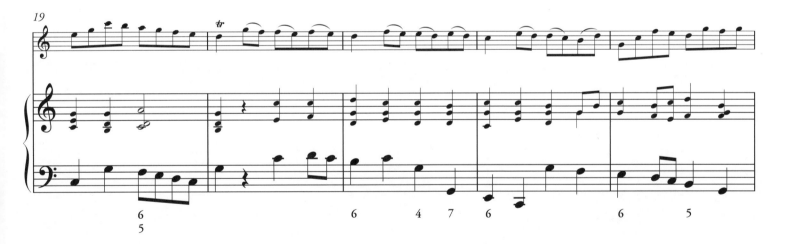

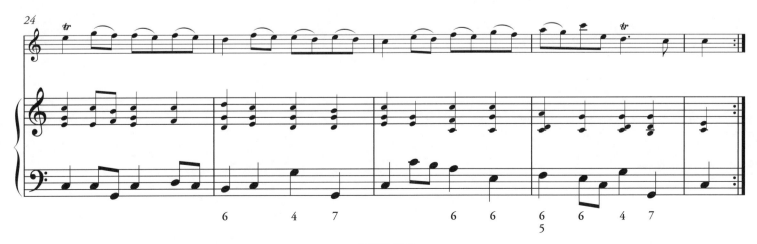

Gracieusement

from "La Simianne"

Ph. de Lavigne

Passacaglia

M. Zimmermann

Recorder

Basso continuo

ENGLISH

DOWANI CD:
- Track No. 1

         $\boxed{1}$ - tuning notes

- Track numbers in circles   ⬤ - concert version

- Track numbers in squares

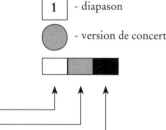

- slow Play Along Tempo
- intermediate Play Along Tempo
- original Play Along Tempo

- Additional tracks for longer movements or pieces
- **Concert version:** recorder and basso continuo
- **Slow tempo:** The recorder can be faded in or out by means of the balance control. Channel 1: recorder solo; channel 2: harpsichord accompaniment with recorder in the background; middle position: both channels at the same volume
- **Intermediate tempo:** basso continuo only
- **Original tempo:** basso continuo only

FRANÇAIS

DOWANI CD :
- Plage N° 1

         $\boxed{1}$ - diapason

- N° de plage dans un cercle   ⬤ - version de concert

- N° de plage dans un rectangle

- tempo lent play along
- tempo moyen play along
- tempo original play along

- Plages supplémentaires pour mouvements ou morceaux longs
- **Version de concert :** flûte à bec et basse continue
- **Tempo lent :** Vous pouvez choisir – en réglant la balance du lecteur CD – entre les versions avec ou sans flûte à bec. 1er canal : flûte à bec solo ; 2nd canal : accompagnement de clavecin avec flûte à bec en fond sonore ; au milieu : les deux canaux au même volume
- **Tempo moyen :** seulement l'accompagnement de la basse continue
- **Tempo original :** seulement l'accompagnement de la basse continue

DEUTSCH

DOWANI CD:
- Track Nr. 1

         $\boxed{1}$ - Stimmtöne

- Trackangabe im Kreis   ⬤ - Konzertversion

- Trackangabe im Rechteck

- langsames Play Along Tempo
- mittleres Play Along Tempo
- originales Play Along Tempo

- Zusätzliche Tracks bei längeren Sätzen oder Stücken
- **Konzertversion:** Blockflöte und Basso continuo
- **Langsames Tempo:** Blockflöte kann mittels Balance-Regler ein- und ausgeblendet werden. 1. Kanal: Blockflöte solo; 2. Kanal: Cembalobegleitung mit Blockflöte im Hintergrund; Mitte: beide Kanäle in gleicher Lautstärke
- **Mittleres Tempo:** nur Basso continuo
- **Originaltempo:** nur Basso continuo

DOWANI - 3 Tempi Play Along is published by:
DOWANI International
A division of De Haske (International) AG
Postfach 60, CH-6332 Hagendorn
Switzerland
Phone: +41-(0)41-785 82 50 / Fax: +41-(0)41-785 82 58
Email: info@dowani.com
www.dowani.com

Recording & Digital Mastering: Wachtmann Musikproduktion, Germany
Music Notation: Notensatz Thomas Metzinger, Germany
Design: Andreas Haselwanter, Austria
Printed by: Zrinski d.d., Croatia
Made in Switzerland

Concert Version
Manfredo Zimmermann, Treble (Alto) Recorder
Mechthild Winter, Harpsichord / Organ

3 Tempi Accompaniment
Slow:
Mechthild Winter, Harpsichord /
Organ

Intermediate:
Mechthild Winter, Harpsichord /
Organ

Original:
Mechthild Winter, Harpsichord /
Organ